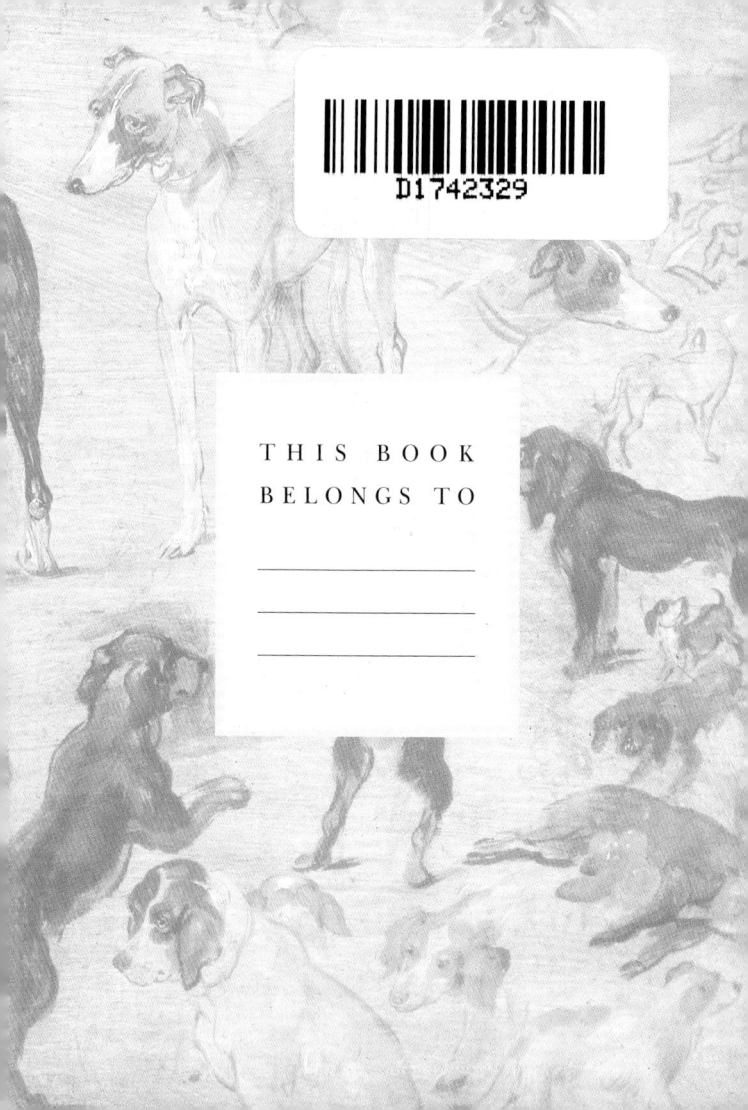

THIS BOOK
BELONGS TO

_____

_____

_____

DOGS

IN WORDS AND PICTURES

FOUR SEASONS
PUBLISHING LIMITED

DOGS

Dogs laugh,
but they laugh with their tails.

MAX EASTMAN

To his dog, every man is Napoleon;
hence the constant popularity of dogs.

ALDOUS HUXLEY

Lots of people have a rug,
Very few have a pug.

E.B. WHITE

Animals are such agreeable friends –
They ask no questions, they pass no criticisms.

GEORGE ELIOT

WHEN THE CAT'S AWAY THE MICE WILL PLAY

Philip Eustace Stretton fl. 1879–1919

Who loves me
will love my dog also.

ST BERNARD

I like a bit of a mongrel myself,
whether it's a man or a dog:
they're the best for everyday.

BERNARD SHAW

If you pick up a starving
dog and make him prosperous
he will not bite you.
That is the principal difference
between a dog and a man.

MARK TWAIN

POINTERS IN A LANDSCAPE

Harrington Bird fl.1870–1893

DIGNITY AND IMPUDENCE
Sir Edwin Landseer 1802–1873

No man is so poor that
he can't afford to keep one dog,
and I've seen them so poor that
they could afford to keep three.

JOSH BILLINGS

There is sorrow enough
   in the natural way
From men and women to fill our day;
And when we are certain
   of sorrow in store
Why do we always arrange for more?
Brothers and Sisters, I bid you beware
Of giving your heart to a dog to tear.

RUDYARD KIPLING

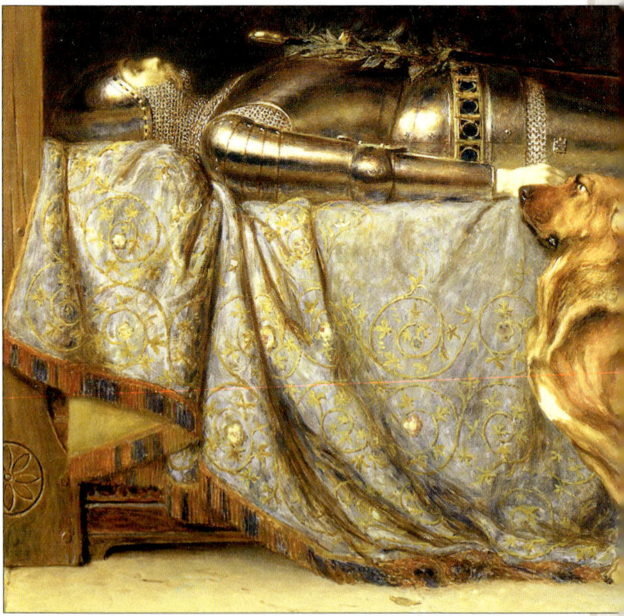

REQUIESCAT

Briton Riviere 1840–1920

DOGS

My little old dog;
A heart-beat. At my feet.

EDITH WHARTON

A dog is the only
thing on earth
that loves you more
than you love yourself.

JOSH BILLINGS

At thieves I bark'd,
at lovers wagg'd my tail,
And thus I pleased both
Lord and Lady Frail.

JOHN WILKES

DOGS

Gentlemen of the jury;
the one absolutely unselfish friend
that man can have in this selfish world,
the one that never deserts him,
the one that never proves ungrateful
or treacherous, is his dog.

SENATOR GEORGE GRAHAM VEST

The great pleasure of a dog
is that you may make a fool of yourself
with him and not only will he not scold
you, he will make a fool of himself too.

SAMUEL BUTLER

A door is what a dog
is perpetually on the wrong side of.

OGDEN NASH

WHIPPET BELONGING TO
FRIEDRICH THE GREAT
Anonymous

TERRIERS RATTING IN A BARN
George Armfield fl. 1840–1884

DOGS

A dog desires affection
more than its dinner. Well – almost.

CHARLOTTE GRAY

Most dog owners are at length able
to teach themselves to obey their dog.

ROBERT MORLEY

Man is an animal that makes bargains;
no other animal does this – no dog exchanges
bones with another.

ADAM SMITH

The Old Dog's Philosophy:
An old dog saw a pup
chasing its tail and asked,
"Why are you chasing your tail?"

Said the puppy, "I have mastered philosophy;
I have solved the problems of the universe
which no dog before me had rightly solved;
I have learned that the best thing
for a dog is happiness,
and that happiness is my tail.
Therefore I am chasing it;
and when I catch it, I shall have it!"

Said the old dog: "My son, I, too,
have paid attention to the problems
of the universe in my weak way,
and have formed some opinions.
I, too, have judged that happiness
is a fine thing for a dog,
and that happiness is in my tail.

DOGS

SEALYHAM PUPPIES AND DUCKLINGS
Lilian Cheviot fl.1894–1902

But I have noticed that when I chase it,
it keeps running away from me;
but when I go about my business,
it comes after me."

Quoted in *Sunshine Magazine*

DOGS

AU BORD DE LA MER

François Flameng 1856–1923

A dog teaches a boy fidelity,
perseverance and to turn around
three times before lying down.

ROBERT BENCHLEY

Two dogs were talking.
"What's your name?" asked the first.
"I'm not sure," replied the second,
"but I think it must be 'Down Boy !'"

A HIGHLANDER IN HIS CROFT
Richard Ansdell 1815–1855

The more I see of the representatives
of the people, the more I admire my dogs.

ALPHONSE DE LAMARTINE

A dog is loved by old and young.
He wags his tail, and not his tongue.

Farmer's Almanac

NAUGHTY BOY! OR COMPULSORY EDUCATION
Charles Burton Barber 1845–1894

Every dog is a lion at home.

TORRIANO

It is a common proverb,
"Dogs bark more for custom
than fierceness."

SIR GEORGE WHARTON

The dog is man's best friend,
He has a tail on one end,
Up in front he has teeth,
And four legs underneath.

OGDEN NASH

We are alone, absolutely alone on this chance
plant; and, amid all the forms of life that
surround us, not one, excepting the dog,
has made an alliance with us.

MAURICE MAETERLINCK

Dachshunds are ideal dogs for small children,
as they are already stretched and pulled to such
a length that the child cannot do much harm
one way or the other.

ROBERT BENCHLEY

The most affectionate creature
in the world is a wet dog.

AMBROSE BIERCE

Buy a pup and your
money will buy love unflinching.

RUDYARD KIPLING

MISS RAMSDEN AND HER DOG
Anonymous

Two boys were talking about their respective dogs.

"I can't figure it out," complained one. "How is it that you can teach your dog all those tricks and I can't teach my dog anything at all?"

"Well," said the other boy, "to begin with, you gotta know more than your dog."

Dogs are evidently intended by God
to be our companions, protectors and,
in many ways, examples.

FATHER BERTRAND WILBERFORCE

Man is a dog's ideal
of what God should be.

HOLBROOKE JACKSON

Money will buy a pretty good dog,
but it won't buy the wag of his tail.

JOSH BILLINGS

A SCOTTISH AND A SEALYHAM TERRIER
Lilian Cheviot fl.1894–1902

ALSO IN THIS SERIES

Cats — In Words and Pictures
Golf — In Words and Pictures
Women — In Words and Pictures

Published by

FOUR SEASONS
PUBLISHING LIMITED

16 Orchard Rise, Kingston Upon Thames, Surrey KT2 7EY
Tel: 020 8942 4445
E-mail: info@fourseasons.net

Text research by *Pauline Barrett*
Designed in association with *The Bridgewater Book Company*
Picture research by *Vanessa Fletcher*
Printed in Singapore

ISBN 1-85645-505-X

ACKNOWLEDGEMENTS

Four Seasons Publishing Ltd would like to thank all those
who kindly gave permission to reproduce the words and visual
material in this book; copyright holders have been identified
where possible and we apologise for any inadvertent omissions.

We would particularly like to thank the following
for the use of pictures: *Bridgeman Art Library, e.t. archive,
Fine Art Photographic Library.*

Front Cover: THE FIRST TASTE, *Carter and Lucas*
Title Page: MISS RAMSDEN AND HER DOG, *Anonymous*
Endpaper: STUDY OF HOUNDS, *Jan Brueghel 1568–1625*
Frontispiece: A DOG'S DINNER, *George Earl* fl. 1856–1883
Back Cover: DIGNITY AND IMPUDENCE, *Sir Edwin Landseer 1802–1873*